WE HAVE LOTS OF FRIENDS

TROY B. WILLIAMS

Here is an <u>AGGREGATION</u> of manatees.

Mom does not like the ARMY of ants when they are in her kitchen.

There is an ARMY of frogs that live in my grandmas pond.

Turtles in a group are a <u>NEST.</u>

This is a **<u>BAND</u>** of gorillas.

A TROOP of monkeys can
also be called a BARREL

This is a BATTERY of barracuda.

A _BEVY_ of swans is beautiful to see.

Always be careful if there is a _Bloat_ of hippopotami close by.

LAST NIGHT WE HEARD A CACKLE OF HYENAS CACKLING.

Our Camel friends are part of a <u>CARAVAN.</u>

Yesterday a CLOUD of bats flew over our picnic.

There is a __COLONY__ of rabbits that lives in grandpas garden.

A family of rinos are called a CRASH.

A group of donkeys is called a DROVE of donkeys.

Our panda friends call their family an EMBARRASSMENT OF PANDA.

We wish we could swim with a FEVER of stingrays.

A FLAMBOYANCE of flamingos is a wonderful sight.

A GANG of turkeys visits us every morning.

This is the GAZE of raccoons that
lives in the tree in my backyard.

We like to chase a KALEIDOSCOPE of butterflies through the fields.

This is a **<u>LABOR</u>** of moles.

If you see a family of leopards it is called a
LEAP of leopards.

Luckily a MOB of emus
can't fly

When on vacation we met a __MOB__ of kangaroos.

There is a MUSTERING o
storks that lives in my
grandmas pond.

OUR FRIENDS THE BUFFALO ARE GATHERED IN AN OBSTINANCY.

Wolves hunt for food in a PACK.

A PADDLING of ducks stops by every year while flying south.

SOMETIMES WE GET A VISIT FROM A PANDAMONIUM OF PARROTS.

SOMETIMES WE GET A VISIT FROM A PANDAMONIUM OF PARROTS.

ONE DAY WE SAW A PARADE OF ELEPHANTS.

a PARLIAMENT of owls asks us questions every night befor bed

Sometimes we pretend to be a <u>POD</u> of dolphins.

We get visits from a PRICKLE of porkupines.

The king of the jungle keeps watch over his **PRIDE** of lions.

We are always careful when we see a RAFT of crocodiles.

When otters get together they are called a RAFT of otters.

We like to watch the SCURRY of squirrels play in the neighborhood trees.

I met a SHIVER of sharks when we went to Hawaii.

We met a **SHREWDNESS** of apes while hiking in the jungle.

A GROUP OF BEARS WOULD BE CALLED A SLEUTH OF BEARS.

We saw a SMACK of jelleyfish when we visited the aquarium

A group of skunks is called a <u>STENCH</u>.

A <u>TOWER</u> of giraffes is an impressive sight.

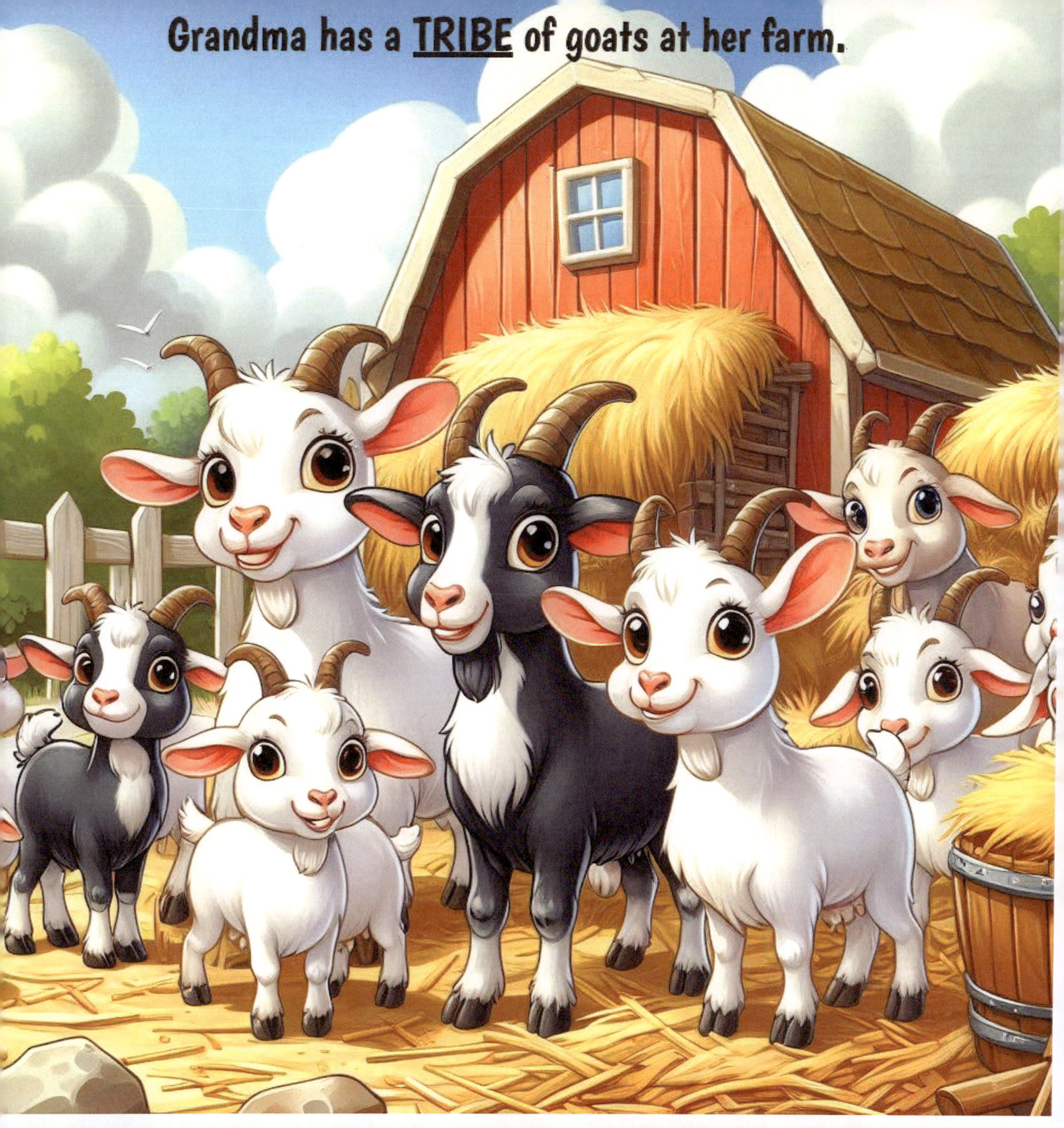
Grandma has a TRIBE of goats at her farm.

It is always fun when A <u>TROOP</u> of baboons comes over for lunch.

An UNKINDNESS of ravens
wakes me up every morning.

We sometimes see a **VENUE** of vultures circling above.

This is a wonderful ZEAL of zebras.